C000203539

DAYS
WITH
LENIN

by Maxim Gorky

University Press of the Pacific
Honolulu, Hawaii

Days with Lenin

by
Maxim Gorky

ISBN: 1-4102-1196-7

Copyright © 2004 by University Press of the Pacific

University Press of the Pacific
Honolulu, Hawaii
http://www.universitypressofthepacific.com

In order to make original editions of historical works
available to scholars at an economical price, this
facsimile of the original edition is reproduced from
the best available copy and has been digitally
enhanced to improve legibility, but the text remains
unaltered to retain historical authenticity.

DAYS WITH LENIN

By Maxim Gorky

Vladimir Lenin is dead. That in him the world has
lost a surpassing genius, one far greater than any of his
great contemporaries, even some of his enemies have
had the courage to admit. The following words form
the conclusion of an article on Lenin, which appeared
in the *Präger Tageblatt,* a German bourgeois newspaper
published in Czechoslovakia—an article whose domi-
nant note is one of awe and reverence for his colossal
figure: "Great and terrible and beyond our comprehension, even in death—such is Lenin." It is clear that
the feeling behind this article is not one of mere gloat-
ing, not the feeling which finds cynical expression in
the saying that "the corpse of an enemy always smells
good"; neither is it the feeling of relief which comes
from the departure of a great but restless spirit. It is
unmistakably the pride of humanity in a great man.

The Russian emigré press had neither the moral courage nor the good taste to express, on the occasion of
Lenin's death, the respect which the bourgeois papers
showed in appreciating the personality of a man whose
life was one of the greatest examples of fearless reason
and resolute will to live.

It would be a difficult task to paint the portrait of
Vladimir Ilyitch * Lenin. His words were as much

---

* Ilyitch—Lenin's patronimic by which his close friends and comrades always liked to refer to him.—*Ed.*

3

a part of his external appearance as scales are of fish. The simplicity and straightforwardness of everything he said were an essential part of his nature. The heroic deeds which he achieved are surrounded by no glittering halo. His was that heroism which Russia knows well—the unassuming, austere life of self-sacrifice of the true Russian revolutionary intellectual who, in his unshakable belief in the possibility of social justice on the earth, renounces all the pleasures of life in order to toil for the happiness of mankind.

What I wrote about him directly after his death, when I was overwhelmed with grief, was hastily written and inadequate. There were things which I could not write then because of considerations of tact, which, I hope, are fully comprehensible. He was a man of piercing vision and great wisdom and "in much wisdom there is much grief."

He could always see a long way ahead, and in discussing people in the years between 1919 and 1921 he often gave an accurate forecast of what they would become in the course of several years. These forecasts were not always flattering, and one did not always want to believe them, but unfortunately in many cases his skeptical remarks have been justified.

The First Meeting

The unsatisfactory character of my former reminiscences was increased by the presence of many bad gaps and inconsistencies. I ought to have begun with the London Congress,* when the figure of Vladimir

* The Congress of the Russian Social-Democratic Labor Party, held in London in 1907.—Ed.

Ilyitch stood out in strong relief against a background of doubt and mistrust, of open hostility and even of hate.

I still see vividly before me the bare walls of a wooden church on the outskirts of London, unadorned to the point of absurdity, the lancet windows of a small, narrow hall which might have been a classroom in a poor school.

Any resemblance to a church was restricted to the outside of the building. Inside there was no trace of anything ecclesiastical and even the low pulpit, instead of standing at the far end of the hall, was placed at the entrance, midway between the two doors.

I had never met Lenin before this, nor read as much of him as I ought to have done. But what I had managed to read, and above all the enthusiastic accounts of those who knew him personally, had attracted me strongly towards him. When we were introduced, he shook me heartily by the hand, and, scrutinizing me with his keen eyes and speaking in the tone of an old acquaintance, he said jocularly: "So glad you've come. I believe you're fond of a scrap? There's going to be a fine old scuffle here."

I did not expect Lenin to be like that. Something was lacking in him. He rolled his "r's" gutturally, and had a jaunty way of standing with his hands somehow poked up under his armpits. He was somehow too ordinary, did not give the impression of being a leader. As a literary man, I am obliged to take note of such little details, and this necessity has become a habit, sometimes even an irritating habit, with me. G. V. Plekhanov, at our first meeting, stood with folded arms, looking at me with the severe, slightly bored expression with which an overworked teacher regards an additional pupil. Nothing that he said has remained in my memory except the extremely trite remark: "I am an admirer of your work"; and neither of us, during the whole time of the Congress, felt any desire to have a heart-to-heart talk with the other.

Before me now stood a baldheaded, stocky, sturdy person, speaking with a guttural roll of his "r's," and holding my hand in one of his, while with the other he wiped a forehead which might have belonged to Socrates, beaming affectionately at me with his strangely bright eyes.

He began at once to speak about the defects of my book *Mother*—evidently he had read it in the manuscript which was in the possession of S. P. Ladyzhnikov. I was hurrying to finish the book, I said,—but did not succeed in saying why. Lenin with a nod of assent, himself gave the explanation: Yes, I should hurry up with it, such a book is needed, for many of the workers who take part in the revolutionary movement do so unconsciously and chaotically, and it would be very useful to them to read *Mother*. "The very book for the moment." This was the single compliment he paid me, but it was a most precious one to me.

Then he went on to ask in a businesslike way, if it was being translated, whether it had been mangled much by the Russian and American censorship. When I told him that the author was to be prosecuted, at first he frowned, then threw back his head, closed his eyes and burst into an unusual laugh. This laugh attracted the workers and F. Uralsky, I think it was, came up, and three other people.

I was in a festive mood. I was in the midst of three hundred picked Party men, who, I learnt, had been sent to the Congress by one hundred and fifty thousand organized workers. Before my eyes were all the Party leaders, the old revolutionaries, Plekhanov, Axelrod, Deutsch. My festive mood was quite natural and will be understood by the reader when I add that I had become extremely low-spirited during the two years I had spent away from my native country.

With the German Social-Democrats

My dejection began in Berlin where I met almost all the leading Social-Democrats, and dined with August Bebel, with Singer, a very stout fellow, beside me, and other distinguished people around.

We dined in a spacious and comfortable room. Tasteful, embroidered cloths were thrown over the canary cages and embroidered antimacassars were fastened on the backs of the armchairs so that the covers should not get soiled from the heads of the persons sitting in them. Everything was solid and substantial. Every one ate in a solemn manner and said to each other in a solemn tone, *"Mahlzeit."* This was a new word for me, but I knew that *"mal"* in French meant "bad," and *"Zeit"* in German meant "time"—"bad times."

Singer twice referred to Kautsky as "my romanticist." Bebel, with his aquiline nose, seemed to me somewhat self-satisfied. We drank Rhenish wine and beer. The wine was sour and tepid. The beer was good. The Social-Democrats spoke sourly and with condescension about the Russian Revolution and Party, but about their own party, the German Party—everything was splendid! There was a general atmosphere of self-satisfaction. Even the chairs looked as though they delighted in supporting the honorable buttocks of the leaders.

My business with the German Party was of a rather delicate nature. A prominent member of it, afterwards the notorious Parvus, had received from *Znaniye* * an authorization to collect author's royalty from the theaters for my play *The Lower Depths*. He received this authorization in 1902 in Sebastopol, at the station, whither he had come on an illegal visit. The money which he collected was to be divided up in the following way: 20 per cent of the total sum to him, and of the rest, I was to receive one quarter, while three quarters went to the funds of the Social-Democratic Party. Parvus knew these conditions, of course, and was even delighted with them. For four years the play had been going the round of all the theaters in Germany, in Berlin alone it had been performed more than 500 times, and Parvus must have collected a hundred thousand marks. But instead of the money, he sent to *Znaniye*, to K. P. Piatnitsky, a letter in which he good-humoredly informed him that he had spent all the money on a trip with a young lady to Italy. As I was concerned personally with this doubtless very pleasant trip only to the extent of a quarter of the money, I considered myself justified in writing to the Central Committee of the German Party about the remaining

---

* A legal publishing house of the Bolsheviks.—*Ed.*

three-quarters. I communicated with them through S. P. Ladyzhikov. The Central Committee remained quite unmoved by Parvus' trip. Later I learnt that he had been degraded by the Party; frankly speaking, I would have preferred to see his ears pulled for him. When I was in Paris some time later, an extremely pretty young woman was pointed out to me as Parvus' companion on his Italian trip. "A very dear young lady," I thought, "very dear."

I met many people in Berlin—writers, artists, patrons of art and letters, and others. Their complacency and self-esteem differed only in degree.

A Trip to America

In America I had seen a lot of Morris Hillquit, whose ambition it was to become mayor or governor of New York. I had seen many people and many things, but I had not met a single person who could understand the whole significance of the Russian Revolution, and I felt everywhere that it was regarded generally as "a mere incident in European life" and a usual occurrence in a country "where there was always either cholera or revolution" in the words of one "beautiful lady" who "sympathized with Socialism."

The idea of a journey to America to collect money for the Bolshevik funds came from L. B. Krassin. V. V. Vorovsky was to go with me as secretary and organizer of meetings. He knew English well, but the Party gave him some other work to do and N. E. Burenin took his place. He did not know the language and began to learn it on the way and when he arrived in the country.

The Socialist-Revolutionaries became childishly interested in my journey when they learnt its purpose. Tchaikovsky and Zitlovsky came to me while I was still in Finland and suggested that money should be collected not for the Bolsheviks, but for "the revolution in general." I refused to collect money for any "general revolution." Then they sent "Babushka" * there also, and so two people appeared in America, who, independently of each other and even without meeting, began to collect money, apparently for two different revolutions.

The Americans of course had neither the time nor inclination to consider which was the better and the more substantial. "Babushka" apparently was already known to them—she had been well advertised in the past by her American friends—and the tzarist embassy prepared a scandal for me.** The American comrades also regarded the Russian Revolution as a "local" and abortive affair and treated somewhat "liberally" the money which I collected at the meetings, and on the whole I collected very little money, less than $10,000. I decided to get some money by writing in the newspapers—but there happened to be a Parvus in America as well, and the American tour was on the whole a failure. However I wrote *Mother* there—a fact which accounts perhaps for its faults and defects.

After that I went to Italy, to Capri, and plunged into

* "Babushka" Catherine Breshkovskaya was called by her followers "grandmother" of the Russian Revolution. She was a social-patriot during the war, supported Kerensky and after the October Revolution became one of the most venomous enemies of the Soviet Union.—*Ed.*

** As soon as Gorky's mission became known, a campaign of social boycott was organised against him presumably on account of his marital relations. He was forced to leave his hotel and seek the hospitality of a friend.—*Ed.*

reading Russian books and newspapers—this also increased my low spirits. If a tooth could feel after being knocked out, it would probably feel as lonely as I did. I was full of amazement at the acrobatic skill and agility with which well-known people jumped from one political platform to another.

"Everything is lost," they said. "They have crushed, annihilated, exiled, imprisoned everybody!"

Much of it was ludicrous, but there was no ray of cheerfulness. One visitor from Russia, a talented writer, said that I had been playing a rôle similar to that of Luke in *The Lower Depths*—had come and charmed the young people with amiable words, they had believed me, had got some knocks on the head, and I had run away. Another declared that I was eaten up by "tendencies," that I was a "played-out" man, and denied any significance to the ballet only because it was "imperial." On the whole they said a lot of stupid and ridiculous things, and I often felt as if a pestilential dust were blowing from Russia.

Then suddenly, as though in a fairy tale, I found myself at the Congress of the Russian Social-Democratic Party. Of course it was a great day for me!

At the London Congress

But my festive mood lasted only until the first meeting when they began wrangling about "the order of the day." The fury of these disputes at once chilled my enthusiasm, and not so much because I felt how sharply the Party was divided into reformers and revolutionaries—I had realized that in 1903—but because of the hostile attitude of the reformers to Lenin. It oozed and spouted out of their speeches like water under high pressure out of an old hose.

It is not always what is said that is important, but how it is said. When Plekhanov, in a frock coat, closely buttoned up like a Protestant pastor, opened the Congress, he spoke like a preacher confident that his ideas are incontrovertible, every word and every pause of great value. Way above the heads of the delegates he skillfully weighed out his beautifully rounded phrases, and whenever any one on the Bolshevik benches uttered a sound or whispered to a comrade, the venerable orator made a slight pause and sent his glance into him like a needle. One of the buttons on his frock coat was a great favorite with Plekhanov; he stroked it caressingly all the time with his finger, and when he paused, pressed it like an electric bell—it seemed to be this pressure which interrupted the flowing current of his speech.

Once at a meeting Plekhanov, rising to answer some one, folded his arms and gave a loud and contemptuous "Ha!" This evoked a laugh among the Bolshevik workers. Plekhanov raised his eyebrows and his cheek grew pale. I say his cheek, for I was sitting at the side of the pulpit and could see the orator's face only in profile.

While Plekhanov was speaking at the first meeting, the person who did the most fidgeting on the Bolshevik benches was Lenin. At one time he hunched himself up as though he were cold, then he sprawled as if he felt hot. He poked his fingers in his armholes, rubbed his chin, shook his head, and whispered something to M. P. Tomsky. When Plekhanov declared that there were no "revisionists" * in the Party, Lenin bent down, the bald spot on his head grew red, and his shoulders shook with silent laughter. The workers sitting next to him and behind him also smiled, and from the back of the hall a voice called out loudly and morosely: "And what about the people sitting over there?"

Little Theodore Dan spoke like a man whose relationship to the authentic truth is one of father and daughter—he has begotten and fostered it, and still fosters it. He is Karl Marx incarnate, and the Bolsheviks—half-educated, ill-mannered children, a fact which is quite clear from their relations with the Mensheviks among whom are to be found, he said, "all the most eminent Marxist thinkers."

"You are not Marxists," he said disdainfully. "No, you are not Marxists"—and he thrust out his yellow fist. One of the workers asked him: "When are you going to tea again with the Liberals?"

I don't remember if it was at the first meeting that Martov spoke. This amazingly attractive man spoke with the ardor of youth and was evidently especially deeply affected by the tragic drama of the dissension and split. He trembled all over, swayed backward and forward spasmodically unfastening the collar of his starched shirt and waving his hands about. His cuff fell down from under the sleeve of his coat, he raised his arm high up and shook it to send the cuff back again to its proper place. Martov did not give so much the impression of ar-

* Supporters of the reformist Bernstein's attempts to "revise" Marxism. —*Ed.*

guing as of urging and imploring: we must put an end
to the split, the Party is too weak to be divided, the
workers must get freedom before anything else, we
mustn't let them lose heart. At times, during the first
part of his speech he sounded almost hysterical; he became obscure through abundance of words, and he
himself gave a painful impression. At the end of his
speech, and without any apparent connection with it,
he began in the same "militant" tone and with the
same ardor, to shout against the militant group and
against all work directed to the preparation of an
armed uprising. I remember distinctly that some one
from the Bolshevik benches cried out, "Well, there you
are!" and Tomsky, I think it was, said: "Have we got
to cut our hands off for Comrade Martov's peace of
mind?"

Again, I do not remember exactly if Martov spoke
at the first meeting. I only mention it in order to de-
scribe the different ways in which people spoke.

After his speech there was a gloomy discussion
among the workers in the room which led into the
hall of the meeting. "There's Martov for you; and he
was one of the 'Iskra' group!" * "Our intellectual
friends are changing their color!"

Rosa Luxemburg spoke eloquently, passionately and
trenchantly, using irony with great effect.

Lenin Speaks

But now Vladimir Ilyitch hurries to the pulpit, and
cries "Comrades!" in his guttural way. He seemed to

---

* From 1900 to 1903 the *Iskra*, with Lenin at its head, was the leading organ of the Russian Social-Democracy. After Lenin's resignation

me to speak badly, but after a minute I and everybody else were absorbed in his speech. It was the first time I had heard complicated political questions treated so simply. There was no striving after eloquent phrases with him, but every word was uttered distinctly, and its meaning was marvelously plain. It is very difficult to pass on to the reader the unusual impression which he made.

His arm was extended with the hand slightly raised, and he seemed to weigh every word with it, and to sift out the remarks of his opponents, substituting them by momentous arguments for the right and duty of the working class to go its own way, and not along with the liberal bourgeoisie or trailing behind it. All this was unusual, and Lenin seemed to say it not of his own will, but by the will of history.

The unity, completeness, directness and strength of his speech, his whole appearance in the pulpit, was a veritable work of classic art: everything was there, and yet there was nothing superfluous, and if there were any embellishments, they were not noticed as such, but were as natural and inevitable as two eyes in a face or five fingers on a hand.

He gave a shorter speech than the orators who spoke before him, but he made a much greater impression. I was not alone in feeling this. Behind me was an enthusiastic whispering: "Now, he has got something to say." It really was so. His conclusions were not reached artificially, but developed by themselves, inevitably. The Mensheviks made no attempt to hide

in November, 1903, it continued publication until 1905 as the organ of the Mensheviks.—*Ed.*

their displeasure at the speech and more than displeasure at Lenin himself. The more convincingly he showed the necessity to the Party of the utmost development of revolutionary theory so that the practice might be thoroughly surveyed in the light of it, the more exasperatedly did they interrupt him.

"A Congress isn't the place for philosophy!" "Don't act the teacher with us, we're not school-boys!"

One tall, bearded individual who looked like a shop-keeper was especially aggressive. He jumped up from his seat and stuttered: "Little p-plots—p-playing at little p-plots! Blanquists!"

Rosa Luxemburg nodded her head in approval of Lenin. She made a neat remark to the Mensheviks at one of the later meetings. "You don't stand on Marxism, you sit on it, rather lie down on it."

A malevolent, burning wave of irritability, irony and hatred swept over the hall. The eyes which reflected Lenin showed a hundred different expressions. These hostile thrusts had no noticeable effect on him. He spoke on warmly but deliberately and calmly. I learned what this external calm had cost him a few days later. It was strange and sad to see that such hostility could be roused against him by such a natural thought as that "only by the help of a fully developed theory would the Party be able to see the causes of the dissension in its midst."

The impression formed itself in my mind that each day of the Congress added ever greater power to Vladimir Ilyitch, and made him bolder and more confident. With each day his speeches sounded firmer and the Bolshevik element in the Congress grew more and more uncompromising and inflexible. Next to Lenin, I was moved most of all by the eloquent, vigorous speech of Rosa Luxemburg against the Mensheviks and the crushing, sledge-hammer blows of M. P. Tomsky's speech against the idea of a Labor Congress.

Lenin and the Workers

His free minutes or hours Lenin spent among the workers, asking them about the most petty details of their lives.

"What about their wives? Up to the neck in house-work? But do they manage to learn anything, to read anything?"

Once in Hyde Park a group of workers who had seen Lenin for the first time at the Congress was dis-cussing his conduct there. One of them made a strik-ing remark:

"For all I know there may be other fellows as clever as he in Europe on the side of the workers. But I don't believe you'll find another one who could get you on the spot like that fellow!"

Another one added with a smile, "He's one of us all right."

"Plekhanov's just as much one of us," some one re-plied. The answer I heard just hit the mark—"You feel that Plekhanov's always teaching you, lording it over you, but Lenin's a real leader and comrade." One young fellow said jokingly: "Plekhanov's frock coat is too tight for him."

On one occasion we were on our way to a restaurant, when a worker, a Menshevik, stopped Lenin to ask him a question. Ilyitch dropped behind while the party went on. He entered the restaurant frowning, five minutes later, and said: "Curious that such a simpleton should have got into the Party Congress. He asked me, what was after all the real reason for the discussion. 'This is what it is,' I said to him. 'Your friends want to get into Parliament, while we believe that the working class has got to prepare for a struggle.' I think he understood."

Several of us always had our meals together in the same cheap little restaurant. I noticed that V. Ilyitch ate very little—two or three fried eggs, a small piece of ham, and a mug of thick, dark beer. He obviously took very little care of himself and his amazing care for the workers struck one all the more.

M. F. Andreyeva looked after the canteen, and he would ask her: "What do you think, are the workers getting enough to eat? No? H'm, h'm. Perhaps we can get more sandwiches?"

Once when he came to the inn where I was staying, I noticed him feeling the bedding with a preoccupied air.

"What are you doing?" I asked.

"I'm just looking to see if the sheets are well aired."

At first I didn't understand. Why should he want to know what the sheets were like in London? Then, noticing my perplexity, he explained, "You must take care of yourself."

In the autumn of 1918 I asked a worker from Sormovo, Dmitry Pavlov, what he thought was Lenin's most striking feature. He answered: "Simplicity. He is as simple as truth itself." He said this as though it had been thought out and decided long ago.

It is well known that one's severest critics are those who work under one. Lenin's chauffeur, Gill, a man of great experience, said: "Lenin is quite unique. There are no others like him. Once I was driving him along Myasnitskaya Street when the traffic was very heavy. I hardly moved forward. I was afraid of the car getting smashed and was sounding the horn, feeling very worried. He opened the door, reached me by standing on the footboard, meanwhile running the risk of being knocked down, and urged me to go forward. 'Don't get worried, Gill, go on like every one else.' I am an old chauffeur. I know that nobody else would do that."

It would be difficult to make the reader realize how easily and naturally all his impressions flowed in the same channel. With the invariability of a compass needle his thoughts turned in the direction of the class interests of the workers.

On one of our free evenings in London a small company of us went to a Music Hall.

V. Ilyitch laughed gayly and infectiously at the clowns and comedians and looked indifferently at the rest. He paid special attention to the timber-felling by the workers of British Columbia. The little scene at the back showed a forest camp and on the ground in front two young fellows hewed through the trunk of a tree about a meter in thickness in the course of a minute.

"That's for the public, of course," said Ilyitch.

"They couldn't work as quickly as that in reality. But apparently they use axes there also, and cut up a lot of wood into useless chips. There's British civilization for you!"

He began to speak about the anarchy in production under capitalism, the great percentage of raw material which is wasted, and ended by regretting that no one had as yet thought of writing a book on the subject.

The idea wasn't quite clear to me, but I didn't manage to question V. Ilyitch. He was already making some interesting remarks about the pantomime as a special form of the art of the theater. "It is the expression of a certain satirical attitude towards generally accepted ideas, an attempt to turn them inside out, to distort them, to show the arbitrariness of the usual. It is a little complicated, but interesting!"

Two years later in Capri, when he was discussing the Utopian novel with A. A. Bogdanov, he said, "If you would write a novel for the workers on the subject of how the sharks of capitalism robbed the earth and wasted the oil, iron, timber and coal—that would be a useful book, Signor Machist!" *

A Meeting in Paris

When he said good-by to me in London he promised to come to Capri for a rest. But before he had made up his mind to come, I saw him in Paris in a two-roomed student's flat (it was a student's flat only in size, not in the cleanliness and order that reigned

* Machism was the name given to the tendency at that time to revise Marxism by diluting it with a new version of philosophical idealism based on the mechanist theories of the Austrian physicist Ernst Mach. —Ed.

there). Nadejda Konstantinovna * had gone out after
giving us tea and we remained alone together.

Znaniye had just gone to pieces, and I had come to
discuss with V. Ilyitch the organization of a new publishing house which would embrace as far as possible
all our literary people. I proposed for the editorial
office abroad, V. Vorovsky and some one else, and in
Russia V. A. Dyesnitsky would represent them. I
thought that a series of books should be published on
the history of the literatures of the West and on Russian literature, books on the history of civilization
which would provide the workers with a mine of in-
formation for purposes of self-education and propaganda. But Vladimir Ilyitch quashed the plan by
pointing to the censorship and the difficulty of organizing the people. The majority of the comrades were
occupied with practical Party work—they had no time
for writing. But his chief, and for me, most con-
clusive argument was approximately as follows: There
is no time for writing thick books. A thick book
would be read only by the intelligentsia, who are quite
evidently giving up Socialism for liberalism and it is
not for us to turn them from the path they have
chosen. Newspapers and pamphlets are what we need.
It would be a good thing to renew the *Znaniye* library,
but it would be impossible in Russia because of the
censorship, and here because of transport. We have to
throw scores of hundreds of thousands of pamphlets
into the masses, it would be impossible to convey such
a heap illegally. Let us wait for a publishing house till
better times.

* N. K. Krupskaya, Lenin's wife.—*Ed.*

With his invariably striking vividness and clarity, he began to talk about the Duma and the Cadets * who, he said, are "ashamed to be Octobrists" ** and have only one way open to them, the road to the right. Then he brought forward a series of arguments for the imminence of war and "probably not of one, but of a whole series of wars"; *a prophecy which was speedily fulfilled in the Balkans.* He got up and with characteristic gesture, putting his thumbs in his waistcoat armholes, paced slowly up and down the little room, screwing up his bright eyes, said:

"War is coming. It is inevitable. The capitalist world has reached the stage of putrescent fermentation. People are already beginning to poison themselves with the drugs of chauvinism and nationalism. I think we shall yet see a general European war.

"The proletariat? The proletariat will hardly be able to find in itself the strength to avert the carnage. How could it be done? A general strike of workers all over Europe? They are not yet sufficiently organized or class-conscious for that. Such a strike would be the signal for a civil war but we as practical politicians cannot count on that."

He paused, scraping the soles of his shoes on the floor, then said gloomily: "The proletariat of course will suffer terribly. Such must be its fate for some time yet. But its enemies will weaken each other, that also is inevitable."

Coming up to me he said forcibly but not loudly,

* Members of the bourgeois-liberal Constitutional Democratic Party. —*Ed.*

** The party of big capital and landowners.—*Ed.*

as if in amazement: "No, but think of it. Why should people who are well-fed force hungry ones to fight against each other? Could you name a more idiotic or more revolting crime? The workers will pay a dreadfully heavy price for this, but in the end they will gain. It is the will of history."

He often spoke of history but I never felt in what he said any fetishistic worship of its will or power.

His words had agitated him. He sat down and, wiping the sweat from his forehead, drank a little cold tea and asked unexpectedly: "What was that affair of yours in America? I know from the newspapers what it was about, but how did it end?"

I briefly related my adventures. I have never met a man who could laugh so infectiously as Lenin. It was strange to see such a stern realist, a man who saw so well, and felt so deeply, the inevitability of great social catastrophes, irreconcilable, relentless in his hatred towards the capitalist world, laughing like a child, till the tears came, till he choked with laughter. To laugh like that one must have the soundest and healthiest of minds.

"Oh, you are a—humorist!" he said through his laughter. "I would never have thought that anything could be so funny."

Wiping his eyes, he was at once serious, and said with his kind, soft smile: "It's a good thing that you can meet failure with humor. Humor is a splendid, healthy quality. And really life is as funny as it is sad, just as much."

We agreed that I should visit him in a day's time,

but the weather was bad and I began spitting a good deal of blood in the evening and left the next day.

Lenin in Italy

The next time we met after Paris was in Capri. I had a very strange impression at that time—as though V. Ilyitch were twice in Capri and in two sharply different moods. One Ilyitch, when I met him at the wharf, immediately declared to me resolutely: "I know A. M. that you are always hoping that it will be possible to reconcile me with the Machists although I warned you of the futility of it in a letter. So don't make any attempts."

I tried to explain to him on the way to my lodgings and afterwards, that he was not absolutely right. I never have had, nor have I now, any intention of reconciling opposing philosophies which, by the way, I do not understand very well. In addition I had been mistrustful of all philosophies from my youth, and the cause of this mistrust had always been the contradiction between philosophy and my personal "subjective" experience. For me the world had only just begun, it was in the process of becoming, but philosophy gave it a slap on the head and put to it the entirely misplaced and irrelevant question: "Whither are you going? Wherefore are you going? Why do you think?" Some philosophers give the simple, stern command, "Stop!" In addition, I was aware that philosophy, like a woman, can be very plain, even hideous, but dressed up so skillfully and convincingly that she can be taken for a beauty.

This made V. Ilyitch laugh. "Well, that's making a

joke of it," he said. "That the world is only beginning, is in process of becoming—well, think it over seriously. You will come from that point to the place where you ought to have come long ago."

Then I told him that in my eyes A. A. Bogdanov, A. Lunacharsky and V. A. Bazarov were important people, highly and thoroughly educated, and had no equals in the Party.

"Granted. Well, what follows?"

"I consider them to be people aiming finally at the same thing, and if profoundly understood and realized, the unity of their aim should wipe out and annihilate philosophical contradictions."

"That means that the hope of reconciliation is still alive after all? It is quite useless," he said. "Put it out of your head, as completely as possible, I advise you as a friend. Plekhanov, according to you, has the same aim as well, and I, between ourselves, consider that he has quite another aim, although he is a materialist and not a metaphysician."

Our conversation ended here. There is no need, I think, to say that I have not reproduced it in exactly the original words. But I am quite sure of the accuracy of the ideas.

So Vladimir Ilyitch Lenin stood before me even more firm and more inflexible than at the London Congress. But then he was agitated, then there were times when the Party split clearly made him live through some painful moments. Now he was in a calm, rather cold and satirical mood, sternly putting aside all philosophical themes, and continually on the alert.

A. A. Bogdanov, who was an extremely attractive person, of a very mild character and very fond of Lenin, though with a rather high opinion of himself, had to listen to these biting and painful words: "Schopenhauer said that 'clear thinking means clear speaking' and I think he never said a truer word. You don't explain yourself clearly, Comrade Bogdanov. Explain to me in a few words what your 'substitution' will give to the working class, and why Machism is more revolutionary than Marxism?"

Bogdanov tried to explain but he really did speak in a confused and wordy fashion.

"Drop it," advised V. Ilyitch. "Somebody or other, Juares, I think, said, 'It is better to speak the truth than to be a minister'—or a Machist, I would add." Then he plunged into a game of chess with Bogdanov, and when he lost grew angry and even despondent like a child. It is worthy of remark that even this childish despondency, like his astonishing laugh, did not impair the completeness and unity of his character.

There was in Capri another Lenin—a splendid comrade, a light-hearted person with a lively, inexhaustible interest in everything in the world, and strikingly gentle. Late one evening when every one had gone out for a walk, he said to me and M. F. Andreyeva sadly and with deep regret: "Such clever and talented people, who have done a great deal for the Party, and could do ten times more—and they will not go with us! They cannot do so. And scores, hundreds of such people are ruined and mutilated by this criminal régime."

Another time he said: "Lunacharsky will return to

the Party. He is less of an individualist than the other
two. He has a highly gifted nature such as is rarely
met with. I 'have a weakness' for him. What stupid
words, 'to have a weakness!' I am really very fond of
him, you know, he is a splendid comrade! There is
something of the French brilliancy about him. His
levity is the result of his estheticism."

He asked in detail about the life of the Capri fishermen, about their earnings, the influence of the priests,
their schools. I could not but be surprised at the range
of his interests. When a priest was pointed out to him,
the son of a poor peasant, he immediately asked for in-
formation as to how often the peasants send their children to the seminaries, and whether the children
returned to their own village as priests.

"You understand? If this isn't an isolated case, it
means that it is the policy of the Vatican—an artful
policy!"

I cannot imagine another man who, so far surpassing
other people, could yet remain unaffected by ambitious
cravings and retain a lively interest in simple folk.

There was a certain magnetic quality in him which
drew the hearts and sympathies of the working people
to him. He did not speak Italian, but the Capri fishermen, who had seen Chaliapin and many other outstanding Russians, by a kind of instinct put Lenin in a
special place at once. His laugh was enchanting—the
hearty laugh of a man, who through being so well ac-
quainted with the clumsy stupidity of human beings
and the acrobatic trickery of the quick-witted, could
find pleasure in the child-like artlessness of the "simple
in heart." One old fisherman, Giovanni Spadaro, said

of him: "Only an honest man could laugh like that."

We would go rowing sometimes, on water blue and transparent as the sky, and Lenin learned how to catch fish "with his finger"—using the line alone, without the rod. The fishermen explained to him that the fish must be hooked when the finger feels the vibration of the line. *"Cosi: drin, drin. Capisce?"*

A second later he hooked a fish, drew it in and cried out with child-like joy and a hunter's excitement, *"Drin, drin."* The fishermen roared with laughter, gay as children, and nicknamed the fisherman "Signor Drin-Drin." After he had gone away, they continued to ask: "How is Drin-Drin getting on? The Tsar hasn't caught him yet?"

I do not remember if it was before Lenin's visit or after that Plekhanov came to Capri. Some of the emigrants in the Capri colony, the writer Oliger, Lorentz-Mettner, who was condemned to death for organizing the rising in Sotchi, Paul Vigdorchik, and, I think, two others, wanted to speak to him. He refused. He had a right to do so. He was ill and had come for a rest. But Oliger and Lorentz told me that he had refused in a very offensive way. Oliger, who was of a highly-strung temperament, insisted that Plekhanov had said something about "being sick of the crowd of people who all want to speak but are incapable of doing anything." When he was with me, he really did not wish to see any one from the local colony. Ilyitch saw them all. Plekhanov never asked about anything. He already knew it all and told you all about it himself. Talented in the wide Russian way and with a European education, he loved to parade his wit, and for the sake apparently of a pungent jest would lay the cruelest emphasis on the weak points of foreign or Russian comrades. To me his witticisms often appeared pointless and only such have remained in my memory: "Immoderately moderate Mehring; Enrico Ferri is an imposter; there is neither gold nor iron in him." This pun was built up on the word *ferro,* meaning iron. All of them were after this pattern. As a general rule he had a condescending manner towards people, as if he were a god. I felt deep respect for him as a very talented writer and the theoretical inspirer of the Party, but no sympathy. There was too much of the "aristocrat" in him. I may be mistaken in my judgment. I am not fond of indulging in mistakes, but like everybody else cannot always avoid them.

But the fact remains that I have rarely met two people with less in common than G. V. Plekhanov and V. I. Lenin; and this was natural. The one was finishing his work of destroying the old world, the other was beginning the construction of a new.

Life plays such malicious tricks on us, that those who are incapable of real hatred are incapable of real love also. This fact alone, distorting human nature at the root, this unavoidable division of the soul, the inevitability of love through hatred, condemns the modern conditions of life to dissolution.

I have never met in Russia, the country where the inevitability of suffering is preached as the general road to salvation, nor do I know of, any man who hated, loathed and despised so deeply and strongly as Lenin all unhappiness, grief and suffering. In my eyes, these feelings, this hatred of the dramas and tragedies of life exalted Lenin more than anything, belonging as he did to a country where the greatest masterpieces have been gospels in praise and sanctification of suffering, and where youth begins its life under the influence of books which are in essence descriptions of petty, trivial dramas monotonously unvarying. The literature of Russia is the most pessimistic in Europe. All our books are written on one and the same theme—how we suffer in youth and middle-age from our own foolishness, from the oppressive weight of autocracy, on account of women, from love of one's neighbor, from the unsuccessful structure of the universe; how we suffer in old age from consciousness of the mistakes we have made in our lives, from lack of teeth, from indigestion and the imminence of death. Every Russian who has passed a month in prison for some political offense, and a year in exile, considers it his sacred duty to present Russia with a book of reminiscences about his sufferings. But a happy life no one has ever thought of putting into the form of memoirs. As Russians are in the habit of thinking out what their lives shall be, but unable to make them come out that way, maybe such a book would teach them how to devise a happy life.

Lenin was exceptionally great, in my opinion, precisely because of this feeling in him of irreconcilable, unquenchable hostility towards the sufferings of humanity, his burning faith that suffering is not an essential and unavoidable part of life, but an abomination which people ought and are able to sweep away.

Differences with Lenin in 1917

In the years 1917-18 my relations with Lenin were
not what I would have wished them to be, but they
could not be otherwise. He was a politician. He had
to perfection that clear-sighted directness of vision
which is so indispensable in the helmsman of so enormous and heavily burdened a ship as Russia with its
dead-weight of peasants. I have an organic distaste
for politics, and little faith in the reasoning powers of
the masses, especially of the peasants. Reason without
ordered ideas is yet far from being the force which
lives in creative activity. There can be no ideas in the
minds of the mass until the community of interests of
all the separate individuals is realized.

The mass has been striving for thousands of years
towards the good, and this striving engenders rapa-
cious beasts out of the flesh of the mass, which enslave
it and live on its blood. So it will be, until it realizes
that there is only one force which can free it from the
thraldom of the beasts, the force of the truth which
Lenin taught.

When in 1917 Lenin on his arrival in Russia published his theses * I thought that by these theses he was
sacrificing to the Russian peasantry the small but
heroic band of politically educated workers and all
the genuine revolutionaries of the intelligentsia. The
single active force in Russia, I thought, would be
thrown like a handful of salt into the vapid bog of
village life, and would dissolve without leaving any

* An analysis of the nature of the February Revolution and the
Bolshevik program to continue the revolution until the workers in alliance
with the poor peasants have wrested power from the bourgeoisie.—*Ed.*

trace, would be sucked down without effecting any change in the mind, life or history of the Russian people. The professional intelligentsia, in general, the scientists and technicians, were, from my point of view, revolutionaries by nature, and this socialist intelligentsia, together with the workers, were for me the most precious force stored up in Russia. In 1917 I did not see any other force capable of taking power, and organizing the village. But only on condition of complete inner unity could this force, numerically insignificant and split by contradictions, fulfill its rôle. Before them stood a tremendous task—to bring order into the anarchy of the village, to discipline the mind of the peasant, teach him to work rationally, to reorganize his economy, and by such means make the country progress. All this could only be achieved by subjecting the instincts of the village to the reason of the town.

The primary task of the revolution I considered to be the creation of the conditions which would lead to the development of the cultural forces of the country. To this end I offered to organize in Capri a school for workers, and in the years of reaction, from 1907 to 1913, tried as much as I could to raise the spirits of the workers by every possible method. With this end in view immediately after the February Revolution, there was organized the Free Association for the Development and Spread of Positive Science, an institution which aimed on the one hand, at organizing in Russia scientific research institutions, and on the other, at a broad and continuous popularization of scientific and technical knowledge among the workers. At the head of the Association were the eminent scientists and members of the Academy of Sciences, V. A. Steklov, L. A. Tchugayev, Academician Fersman, S. P. Kostytchev, A. A. Petrovsky, and a number of others. The means were being got together with great energy; S. P. Kostytchev had already begun to look for a place for the Institute of Zoölogical and Botanical Research.

In order to make myself quite clear I will add that all my life, the depressing effect of the prevalency of the illiteracy of the village on the town, the individualism of the peasants, and their almost complete lack of social emotions had weighed heavily on my spirits. The dictatorship of the politically enlightened workers, in close connection with the scientific and technical intelligentsia, was, in my opinion, the only possible solution to a difficult situation which the war had made especially complicated by rendering the village still more anarchical. I differed from the Bolsheviks on the question of the value of the rôle of the intelligentsia in the Russian Revolution, which had been prepared by this same intelligentsia to which belonged all the Bolsheviks who had educated hundreds of workers in the spirit of social heroism and genuine intellectuality. The Russian intelligentsia, the scientific and professional intelligentsia, I thought, had always been, was still, and would long be the only beast of burden to drag along the heavy load of Russian history. In spite of all shocks and impulses and stimulation which it had experienced, the mind of the masses of the people had remained a force still in need of leadership from without.

So I thought in 1917—and was mistaken. This page

of my reminiscences should be torn out. But "what has been written by the pen cannot be cut down by the ax"; and "we learn by our mistakes" as V. Ilyitch often repeated. Let the reader know my mistake. It will have done some good if it serves as a warning to those who are inclined to draw hasty conclusions. Of course, after a series of cases of the most despicable sabotaging by a number of specialists, I had no alternative but to change my attitude toward the scientific and technical professionals. Such changes cost something—especially in old age.

The duty of true-hearted leaders of the people is superhumanly difficult. A leader who is not in some degree a tyrant, is impossible. More people, probably, were killed under Lenin than under Thomas Münzer; but without this, resistance to the revolution of which Lenin was the leader would have been more widely and more powerfully organized. In addition to this we must take into account the fact that with the development of civilization the value of human life manifestly depreciates, a fact which is clearly proved by the growth in contemporary Europe of the technique of annihilating people, and the taste for doing so.

I challenge any one to say frankly how far he approves of, and how far he is revolted by, the hypocrisy of the moralists who talk about the bloodthirstiness of the Russian Revolution when they not only showed no pity for the people who were exterminated during the four years of the infamous Pan-European War, but by all possible means fanned the flame of this abominable war to "the victorious end." To-day the "civilized" nations are ruined, exhausted, decaying, and vulgar petty bourgeois philistinism which is common to all races reigns triumphant, there is no escape from its halter and people are being strangled to death.

Much has been said and written about Lenin's cruelty. I have no intention, of course, of doing anything so ridiculously tactless as to defend him against lies and calumny. I know that lying and slandering is a legitimate method in petty bourgeois politics, a usual way of attacking an enemy. It would be impossible to find a single great man in the world to-day who has not had some mud thrown at him. This is known to everybody. Besides this, there is a tendency in all people not only to reduce an outstanding man to the level of their own comprehension, but to roll him beneath their feet in the viscid noisome mud which they have created and call "every day life."

The following incident is for me repulsively memorable. In 1919 there was a congress in Petrograd of "the village poor." From the villages in the north of Russia came several thousands of peasants, some hundreds of whom were housed in the Winter Palace of the Romanovs. When the congress was over, and these people had gone away, it appeared that not only all the baths of the palace, but also a great number of priceless Sèvres, Saxon and oriental vases had been befouled by them for lavatory use. It was not necessary to do this since the lavatories of the palace were in good order and the water system working. No, this vandalism was an expression of the desire to sully and debase things of beauty. Two revolutions and a war have supplied me with hundreds of cases of this lurking, vindictive tendency in people, to smash, deform, ridicule and defame the beautiful. It must not be thought that I emphasize the conduct of the village poor because of my skeptical attitude to the peasants. This is not the case.

This malicious desire to deface things of exceptional beauty is fundamentally the same as the odious tendency to vilify an exceptional man. Anything exceptional prevents people from living as they want to live. People long, if they have any longings, not for any fundamental change in their social habits, but to acquire additional habits. The gist of the wailing and complaining of the majority is, "Do not interfere with the way of living to which we are accustomed!" Vladimir Lenin was a man who knew better than any one else how to prevent people from leading the life to which they were accustomed. The hatred of the world bourgeoisie for him is nakedly and repellently manifest; the livid plague spot of it shows unmistakably. Disgusting in itself, this hatred yet tells us how great and terrible in the eyes of the world bourgeoisie is Vladimir Lenin, the inspirer and leader of the proletarians of the whole world.

His physical body no longer exists, but his voice sounds ever louder and more triumphantly in the ears of the workers of the earth, and already there is no corner of the world where this voice does not rouse the will of the people to revolution, to the new life, to the creation of a world of equal people. With ever-growing confidence, strength and success do those who were the pupils of Lenin and are now the inheritors of his power carry on the great work.

"The Perfectly Fashioned Figure of Truth"

It was the clearly expressed will to live in him, his active hatred of life's abominations, which attracted me to him. I loved the youthful eagerness which he put into everything he did. His movements were light and agile, and his rare but powerful gestures were in full harmony with his speech, sparing as it was in words, in thought abounding. On his slightly Mongolian face glowed and sparkled the keen eyes of a tireless fighter against the lies and sorrows of life—now glowing and burning, now screwed up, now blinking, now ironically smiling, now lashing with anger. The gleam of his eyes made his words more glowing. Sometimes it seemed as if the indomitable energy of his soul flew out in sparks through his eyes, and his words, shot through and through with it, hung shining in the air. His words always gave one the impression of the physical pressure of an irresistible truth.

It was an unusual and extraordinary thing to see Lenin in the park at Gorky,* so much has the idea of him become associated with the picture of a man sitting at the end of a long table and expertly and skillfully guiding the comrades in their work, with the observant eyes of a pilot, smiling and beaming; or standing on a platform with head thrown back, casting clear distinct words to the hushed crowd, before the eager faces of the people thirsting for truth.

His words always brought to my mind the cold glitter of steel shavings. From these words, with amaz-

* A country place near Moscow to which Lenin would retire for rest, where he spent his period of illness and where he died January 21, 1924. —*Ed.*

ing simplicity, there rose the perfectly fashioned figure of truth.

He was venturesome by nature but his was not the mercenary venturesomeness of the gambler. In Lenin it was the manifestation of that exceptional moral courage which can be found only in a man with an unshakable belief in his calling, in a man with a profound and complete perception of his connection with the world, and perfect comprehension of his rôle in the chaos of the world, the rôle of enemy of that chaos.

With equal enthusiasm he would play chess, look through "A History of Dress," dispute for hours with comrades, fish, go for walks along the stony paths of Capri, scorching under the southern sun, feast his eyes on the golden color of the gorse, and on the swarthy children of the fishermen. In the evening, listening to stories about Russia and the country, he would sigh enviously and say, "I know very little of Russia—Simbirsk, Kazan, Petersburg, exile in Siberia and that is nearly all."

He loved fun, and when he laughed it was with his whole body; he was quite overcome with laughter and would laugh sometimes until he cried. He could give to his short, characteristic exclamation, "H'm, h'm," an infinite number of modifications, from biting sarcasm to noncommittal doubt. Often in this "H'm, h'm" one caught the sound of the keen humor which a sharp-sighted man experiences who sees clearly through the stupidities of life.

Stocky and thick set, with his Socratic head and quick eyes, he would often adopt a strange and rather comical posture—he would throw his head back, inclining it somehow on to his shoulder, thrust his fingers under his armpits, in his waistcoat armholes. There was something deliciously funny in this pose, something of a triumphant fighting cock; and at such a moment he beamed all over with joy, a grown-up child in this accursed world, a splendid human being, who had to sacrifice himself to hostility and hatred, so that love might be at last realized.

About Intellectuals and Specialists

I did not meet Lenin in Russia, or even see him from afar, until 1918, when the final base attempt was made on his life.* I came to him when he had hardly regained the use of his hand and could scarcely move his neck, which had been shot through. When I expressed my indignation, he replied, as though dismissing something of which he was tired: "A brawl. Nothing to be done. Every one acts according to his lights."

We met on very friendly terms, but of course there was evident pity in dear Ilyitch's sharp and penetrating glance, for I was one who had gone astray.

After several minutes he said heatedly: "He who is not with us is against us. People independent of the march of events—that is a fantasy. Even if we grant that such people did exist once, at present they do not and cannot exist. They are no good to any one. All, down to the last, are thrown into the whirl of an actuality which is more complicated than ever before.

---

* Dora Kaplan, a Socialist-Revolutionary, made an attempt on Lenin's life in 1918, when he was leaving a factory where he addressed a meeting of workers.—*Ed.*

You say that I simplify life too much? That this simplification threatens culture with ruin, eh?"

Then the ironic, characteristic "H'm, h'm..."

His keen glance sharpened, and he continued in a lower tone: "Well, and millions of peasants with rifles in their hands are not a threat to culture according to you, eh? You think the Constituent Assembly could have coped with that anarchy? You who make such a fuss about the anarchy of the country should be able to understand our tasks better than others. We have got to put before the Russian masses something they can grasp. The Soviets and Communism are simple.

"A union of the workers and intelligensia, eh? Well, that isn't bad. Tell the intelligentsia. Let them come to us. According to you they are true servants of justice. What is the matter then? Certainly, let them come to us. We are just the ones who have undertaken the colossal job of putting the people on its feet, of telling the whole world the truth about life—it is we who are pointing out to the people the straight path to a human life, the path which leads out of slavery, beggary, degradation."

He laughed and said without any trace of resentment: "That is why I received a bullet from the intelligentsia."

When the temperature of the conversation was more or less normal, he said with vexation and sadness: "Do you think I quarrel with the idea that the intelligentsia is necessary to us? But you see how hostile their attitude is, how badly they understand the need of the moment? And they don't see how powerless they are without us, how incapable of reaching the masses.

They will be to blame if we break too many heads."

We almost always discussed this subject when we met. Although in what he said his attitude to the intelligensia remained one of mistrust and hostility, in actuality he always correctly estimated the importance of intellectual energy in the revolutionary process, and seemed to agree that in essence revolution was the eruption of that energy unable to develop regularly in the straightened conditions which it has outgrown.

I remember one occasion when I was with him and three members of the Academy of Sciences. The conversation was about the necessity of reorganizing one of the highest scientific institutions in Petrograd. When he had seen them off Lenin said contentedly: "Now that's all right. Those are clever men. With them everything is simple, everything is strictly formulated. You see at once that these people know exactly what they want. It is simply a pleasure to work with such people. I especially liked S."—he named one of the greatest names in Russian science, and a day later even asked me by telephone: "Ask S. whether he will come and work with us." And when S. accepted the proposal, he was sincerely glad, rubbing his hands together and saying jokingly: "One after another we shall win over all the Russian and European Archimedes, and then the world will have to change whether it wants to or not!"

At the 8th Congress of the Party,* N. I. Bukharin said among other things: "The nation is the bourgeoisie together with the proletariat. To recognize the right

* In 1919.—*Ed.*

of some contemptible bourgeoisie to self-determination is absolutely out of place."

"No, excuse me," retorted Lenin, "it certainly is not out of place. You appeal to the process of the differentiation of the proletariat from the bourgeoisie, but let us wait and see how it will turn out." Then pointing to the example of Germany, and to the slowness and difficulty with which the process of differentiation develops, and declaring that they would never succeed in planting Communism by means of force, he went on to discuss the question of the importance of the intelligentsia in industry, in the army, in the coöperative movement. I quote from *Izvestia,** from the debates of the Congress.

"This question must be decided at the coming Conference with complete definiteness. We can only build up Communism when it has become more accessible to the masses by means of bourgeois science and technique. For this, it is necessary to take over the apparatus from the bourgeoisie, to attract all the specialists to work in this connection. Without the bourgeois specialists it is impossible to increase the forces of production. They must be surrounded by an atmosphere of comradely coöperation, by workers' commissars, by Communists; conditions must be created which will not allow them to break away, but they must be given the possibility of working better than under capitalism, for otherwise this layer which has received its education from the bourgeoisie, will not begin to work. It is impossible to make a whole layer work by main force.

"The bourgeois specialists are used to doing cultural

* Official organ of the Soviet Government.—*Ed.*

work, they carried it on within the framework of the bourgeois régime, that is, they enriched the bourgeoisie by enormous material work and construction and gave a miserable share in this wealth to the proletariat. Nevertheless, they did carry forward the work of culture—that is their profession. In so far as they see that the workers not only value culture but also help to spread it among the masses, they will change their attitude towards us. Then they will be morally won over and not only politically divided from the bourgeoisie.

"We must attract them to our apparatus, and for that must be prepared to make sacrifices. In dealing with the specialists we must not keep to a system of petty vexations. We must give them the best conditions of life possible. That will be the best policy. If yesterday we talked of legalizing the petty bourgeois parties, and to-day arrest Mensheviks and Left Socialist-Revolutionaries, one straight line runs through this changing policy—the rooting out of counter-revolution and the acquisition of the cultural apparatus of the bourgeoisie."

In this splendid expression of a great policy there is far more real, live sense than in all the wailing of the miserable hypocrisy of petty-bourgeois "humanitarianism." Unfortunately, many who should have understood and appreciated this appeal to honest work in coöperation with the working class, have not understood or appreciated it. They have preferred hole and corner sabotage and treachery. After the abolition of serfdom, many of the house-serfs, slaves by nature, also remained to serve their masters in the very stables where they had been wont to flog them.

Revolutionary Tactics

I often used to speak with Lenin about the cruelty of revolutionary tactics and life.

"What do you want?" he would ask in astonishment and anger. "Is it possible to act humanely in a struggle of such unprecedented ferocity? Where is there any place for soft-heartedness or generosity? We are being blockaded by Europe, we are deprived of the help of the European proletariat, counter-revolution is creeping like a bear on us from every side. What do you want? Are we not right? Ought we not to struggle and resist? We are not a set of fools. We know that what we want can only be achieved by ourselves. Do you think that I would be sitting here if I were convinced of the contrary?"

"What is your criterion for judging which blows are necessary and which are superfluous in a fight?" he asked once, after a heated discussion. I could only give a vague poetical answer to this simple question. It would be impossible to answer otherwise, I think.

I often overwhelmed him with requests of a different nature, and often felt that all the bother I went to for various people made Lenin pity me. He would ask, "Don't you think you are wasting your energies on a lot of rubbish?"

But I continued to do what I thought ought to be done, and was not put off when the man who knew who were the enemies of the proletariat looked at me askance, in anger. He would shake his head crushingly and say, "You are compromising yourself in the eyes of the comrades and workers."

I pointed out that comrades and workers, when their passions were roused and they were irritated, not infrequently hold too lightly the life and liberty of valuable people, and that this in my view not only compromised the honest hard work of the revolution by too great, sometimes even senseless, cruelty, but was objectively and strategically bad, as it repelled many important people from participation in the revolution.

"H'm, h'm," Lenin muttered skeptically, and pointed out to me many cases when the intelligentsia betrayed the interests of the workers.

"Many people among us," he said, "go over to the other side and betray us, not only out of cowardice, but because of their self-esteem, because they are afraid of finding themselves in an embarrassing situation, afraid that their beloved theory will suffer when it comes to grips with reality. But we are not afraid of that. There is nothing holy or sacred about theories or hypotheses for us, they serve us only as instruments."

Yet I don't remember a single instance when any request of mine met with a refusal from Ilyitch. If they were not always fulfilled, it was not his fault but the fault of the mechanism in which the clumsy Russian state machine has always abounded, and, let us grant, a certain malicious reluctance to lighten the lot or save the lives of people of worth. Perhaps, too, there were cases of willful harming, which is an enemy as cynical as it is cunning. Revenge and malice are often effective through force of inertia; and of course there are petty persons with unhealthy minds, with a morbid thirst for the delight of contemplating the sufferings of their neighbors.

Once he showed me a telegram, smiling. "They have arrested me again. Tell them to let me go." It was signed Ivan Volny.

"I have read his book. I liked it very much. After reading the first five words I felt at once that here was a man who understood the inevitability of mistakes, who did not get angry, or fly into a rage if he was hurt personally. This is the third time, I think, that he has been arrested. You had better advise him to leave the village or they'll kill him next. Evidently they are not very fond of him there. Advise him. By telegram."

I was often struck by Lenin's readiness to help people whom he considered to be his enemies, and not only readiness to help but even care for their future. One general, for example, a scientist, a chemist, was threatened with death. "H'm, h'm," said Lenin, after listening attentively to my story. "So you think he didn't know that his sons had hidden fire-arms in his laboratory? That seems rather unlikely. But we must leave it for Dzerzhinsky to unravel. He has a keen instinct for the truth."

Several days later he rang me up in Petrograd and said, "We are letting your general go—I think he has already been set free. What does he intend to do?"

"Homoemulsion."

"Yes, yes—carbolic acid. Well, let him boil his carbolic. Tell me if he is in need of anything."

Lenin spoke ironically in order to conceal the joy, which he did not wish to show, of saving a man's life.

Several days later he asked again: "Well, how is the general getting on? Everything arranged?"

In the Petrograd kitchens in 1919 there appeared a very beautiful woman who demanded severely, "Give me a bone for my dogs! I am Princess T."

There was a story that, unable to bear degradation and hunger any longer, she resolved to throw herself in the Neva, but, so it was said, her four dogs, who had an instinctive intuition of her sad intention, ran after her and by their howls and anguish made her renounce her idea of committing suicide. I related this story to Lenin. Looking me up and down with a sidelong glance, screwing up his eyes and then closing them entirely, he said gloomily, "Even if it is all made up, still the idea is not a bad one. A joke of the revolution."

He was silent. Then he got up and, sorting the papers on the table, said thoughtfully: "Yes, those people are in great straits. History is a cruel stepmother, and when it retaliates, it stops at nothing. What is there to say? It is bad for those people. The clever ones among them understand of course that they have been torn up by the roots and will never grow again; and transplantation in Europe won't satisfy the clever ones. You don't think they will strike root there, do you?"

"I don't think they will."

"That means that they will either go our way or attempt to make another intervention."

I asked him: "Does it only seem to me so, or do you really pity people?"

He answered: "I am sorry for the clever ones. We

haven't enough clever people. We are for the most part a talented people, but mentally lazy." Recollecting several comrades who had outlived their class psychology and were working with the Bolsheviks, he spoke of them with astonishing warmth.

Lenin's Qualities

A man of astounding strength of will, Lenin possessed in the highest degree the best qualities and properties of the revolutionary intelligentsia—self-discipline often amounting to self-torture and self-mutilation, in its most extreme form, amounting to a renunciation of art and to the logic of one of L. Andreyev's heroes: "Other people are living hard lives, and therefore I must live a hard life."

In the hard famine year of 1919 Lenin was ashamed to eat the food which was sent to him by comrades, soldiers and peasants from the provinces. When the parcels came to his bleak flat he would frown, grow embarrassed, and hasten to give the flour, sugar and butter to the sick comrades or to those who were weak from lack of food.

Once, when he invited me to dine with him, he said: "I shall give you some smoked fish—it was sent to me from Astrakhan." And with a frown on his Socratic forehead, turning his sharp glance away from me, he added: "They send things to me as though I were a lord! How can I prevent them doing it? If you refuse and don't accept it, they are hurt. And every one around me is hungry."

Entirely without any personal fads, a stranger to tobacco and wine, occupied from morning to night

with complicated and difficult work, he had no thought
of looking after himself, but kept a vigilant eye on
the health of the comrades.

He would sit at his table in his study, talking quickly
and writing without taking pen from paper: "Good
morning. How are you? I am just finishing. There
is a comrade in the village feeling lonely—evidently
tired. He must be cheered up. State of mind is not
the least important thing!"

Once I came to him in Moscow. He asked, "Have
you dined?"

"Yes."

"You are not lying?"

"There are witnesses. I dined in the Kremlin dining
room."

"I heard that the dinners are not good there."

"Not bad, but could be better."

He immediately asked for details. "Why not good?
In what way could they be improved?" He began to
mutter angrily: "Why can't they get an expert cook
there? People work literally until they faint, they
must be fed with good food so that they will eat more.
I know there is very little food to be got, and that bad;
they must get a good cook there." Then he quoted the
opinion of some hygienist about the part played by
seasoning in the processes of eating and digestion. I
asked: "How do you find time to think about such
things?" He retorted with another question, "About
rational feeding?" and by the tone of his voice I understood that my question was out of place.

An old acquaintance of mine, P. A. Skorokhodov,
another Sormovo worker, a tender-hearted man, com-

plained of the painfulness of work in the Tcheka.*
I said to him, "I think that is not the right work for
you. It isn't congenial to you." He agreed sadly,
"Absolutely uncongenial." But after thinking a little,
he said: "But you know Ilyitch too has to stifle his
emotions, and I am ashamed to be so weak."

I knew and still know many workers who had to,
and have to, grit their teeth hard, and stifle their emotions, to overcome their organic "social idealism" for
the sake of the triumph of the cause they are serving.
Did Lenin too have to stifle his emotions? He paid
too little attention to himself to talk about himself to
others; he, more than any one, could keep silent about
the secret agitation of his soul.

Once, however, in Gorky, when he was caressing
some children, he said: "These will have happier lives
than we had. They will not experience much that we
lived through. There will not be so much cruelty in
their lives."

Then, looking into the distance, to the hills where
the village nestled, he added pensively: "And yet I
don't envy them. Our generation achieved something
of amazing significance for history. The cruelty, which
the conditions of our life made necessary, will be understood and vindicated. Everything will be understood,
everything." He caressed the children with great care,
with an especially gentle and tender touch.

Once I came to him and saw *War and Peace* lying
on the table.

"Yes. Tolstoy. I wanted to read over the scene of

* Abbreviated name for the Extraordinary Commission for Combating
Counter-revolution and Sabotage; since the defeat of counter-revolution
renamed State Political Administration (OGPU).—*Ed.*

the hunt, then remembered that I had to write to a comrade. Absolutely no time for reading. Only last night I managed to read your book on Tolstoy."

Smiling and screwing up his eyes, he stretched himself deliciously in his armchair and, lowering his voice, added quickly, "What a Colossus, eh? What a marvelously developed brain! Here's an artist for you, sir. And do you know something still more amazing? You couldn't find a genuine muzhik in literature until this Count came on the scene."

Then screwing up his eyes and looking at me, he asked, "Can you put any one in Europe beside him?" and replied himself, "No one." And he rubbed his hands, laughing contentedly.

I more than once noticed this trait in him, this pride in Russian literature. Sometimes this feature appeared to me strangely foreign to Lenin's nature, appeared even naïve, but I learned to perceive in it the echo of his deep-seated, joyful love for his fatherland. In Capri, while watching how the fishermen carefully disentangle the nets, torn and entangled by the sharks, he observed: "Our men work more quickly." When I cast some doubt on this remark, he said with a touch of vexation, "H'm, h'm. Don't you think you are forgetting Russia, living on this bump?"

V. A. Dyesnitsky-Stroyev told me that he was once traveling through Sweden with Lenin in a train, and looking at a German monograph on Dürer. Some Germans, sitting in the same carriage, asked him what the book was. Later it appeared that they had never heard of their great artist. This almost roused enthusiasm in Lenin, and twice he said to Dyesnitsky proudly: "They don't know their own artists, but we do."

One evening in Moscow, in E. P. Pyeskovskaya's flat, Lenin was listening to a sonata by Beethoven being played by Isaiah Dobrowein, and said: "I know nothing which is greater than the Appassionata; I would like to listen to it every day. It is marvelous superhuman music. I always think with pride—perhaps it is naïve of me—what marvelous things human beings can do!"

Then screwing up his eyes and smiling, he added, rather sadly: "But I can't listen to music too often. It affects your nerves, makes you want to say stupid, nice things, and stroke the heads of people who could create such beauty while living in this vile hell. And now you mustn't stroke any one's head—you might get your hand bitten off. You have to hit them on the head, without any mercy, although our ideal is not to use force against any one. H'm, h'm, our duty is infernally hard!"

When he himself was nearly a sick man, quite worn out, he wrote me, August 9, 1921:

"A. M!

"I sent on your letter to L. B. Kamenev. I am so tired that I am incapable of the slightest work. And you are spitting blood and yet don't go away? That really is disgracefully imprudent. In Europe, in a good sanatorium, you will get well and be able to do something else worth while. Really, really. But here you can neither get well, nor do anything. There is nothing for you here but bother, useless bother. Go

away and get well. Don't be obstinate, I implore you!
"Yours,
"LENIN."

For more than a year, he insisted with astonishing
persistence that I should leave Russia. I was amazed
that, entirely absorbed in work as he was, he should
remember there was a sick person somewhere in need
of rest. He wrote letters like this to different people—
scores, probably.

Attitude Toward Comrades

I have already described his quite exceptional attitude to the comrades, his attention to them, which
penetrated down even to the smallest details of their
lives. But in this feature of his I never caught the note
of that self-interested care which a clever master sometimes exhibits toward an honest and expert work-
man. This was not the case with Lenin. His was the
heartfelt interest of a sincere comrade, the love which
exists between equals. I know that it is impossible to
consider as Lenin's equals even the greatest people in
his Party, but he himself didn't seem to realize this, or
more probably, did not want to realize it. He was
sometimes sharp with people, when arguing with
them, pitilessly ridiculed them, even laughed at them
in a venomous fashion. All this he did. But how
many times, when judging the people whom yesterday
he criticized and rebuked, was there clearly evident the
note of genuine wonder at their talents and moral
steadfastness; at their unflagging labor under the
abominable conditions of 1918-1921, work amid spies

of all countries and parties, amid the plots which
swelled like festering sores on the body of the war-
exhausted country!

They worked without rest, they ate little and badly,
they lived amid ceaseless alarm. But Lenin himself did
not seem to feel the hardness of these conditions, of
the unforeseen dangers of a society which had been
shaken to the very foundations by the murderous
storms of civil strife. Only once did anything like a
complaint escape him, and that was when he was talking with M. F. Andreyeva, in his room.

"What else can we do, dear M. F.? We have no
alternative but to fight. Do we find it hard? Of
course we do! You think it is not hard for me? It
is, and very hard too. But look at Dzerzhinsky. He
is beginning to look like nothing at all. There is nothing to be done about it. It is better to suffer than to
fail."

The only regret he ever expressed in my presence
was: "I am sorry, deeply sorry, that Martov is not with
us. What a splendid comrade he was, what an absolutely sincere man!"

I remember how long and heartily he laughed at
reading Martov's remark somewhere, "There are only
two Communists in Russia, Lenin and Kollontay." He
laughed and then sighed, "What a clever woman she
is!"

It was with genuine respect and wonder that he
remarked, after conducting one comrade, an admin-
istrator, out of his study, "Have you known him for
long? He would be at the head of the cabinet in any

country in Europe." Rubbing his hands and smiling, he added: "Europe is poorer than we are in talent."

Once I proposed that we should go together to the Chief Artillery Department to see an apparatus which had been invented by a Bolshevik, an old artillery man, to adjust artillery fire directed against airplanes. "What do I understand about that?" he said, but he went with me.

In a dark room around a table on which stood the apparatus were gathered seven generals with scowling faces, gray, bewhiskered old men, all scientists. Among them the modest civilian figure of Lenin was lost, dropped into insignificance.

The inventor began to explain the construction of the apparatus. Lenin listened to him for two or three minutes, then said approvingly, "H'm, h'm," and began to question the man with as much ease as if he were examining him on some political question.

"And how do you manage to get the machine to do two things simultaneously, when it is laying the sight? Would it be impossible to form an automatic connection between the mounting of the barrel and the indications of the mechanism?" He asked how far the dangerous space extended, and something else. The inventor and the generals gave eager explanations, and next day the former said to me:

"I had told my generals that you were coming with a comrade, but I didn't say who the comrade was. They didn't recognize Ilyitch and probably would never have imagined that he could appear without a great deal of ceremony or a bodyguard. They asked me, 'Is he a technical engineer or a professor? What? Lenin? What a surprise! How is it possible? How does he know so much about these things we're concerned with? He asked those questions like a technologist.' What mystification!"

Apparently they didn't really believe that it was Lenin. On the way from the Chief Artillery Department, Lenin kept chuckling, and talked about the inventor.

"See how easily you can be mistaken in a man! I knew that he was an honest old comrade, but *qui n'a pas inventé la poudre!* [who has not invented powder]. But that seems to be precisely in his line. Good fellow! And didn't the generals go for me when I expressed my doubts as to the practical value of the apparatus? And I did it on purpose, wanted to know what they thought of the ingenious contrivance."

He shook with laughter, then asked: "Tell me, has I. any more inventions to his credit? Well, he oughtn't to work at anything else. Ah, if only we could give all these technical engineers ideal conditions for their work! In twenty-five years Russia would be the foremost country of the world."

Yes, he often praised the comrades in my hearing, even those with whom he was not personally in sympathy. Lenin knew how to appreciate their energy. I was very surprised at his high appreciation of L. D. Trotsky's organizing abilities. V. Ilyitch noticed my surprise.

"Yes, I know there are lying rumors about my attitude to him. But what is, is, and what isn't, isn't—

DAYS WITH LENIN 57

that I know also. He was able at any rate to organize the military experts."

After a pause he added in a lower tone, and rather sadly: "And yet he isn't one of us. With us, but not of us. He is ambitious. There is something of Lassalle in him, something which isn't good."

These words, "with us, but not of us," he used twice in my hearing, the second time about another prominent man, who died soon after V. Ilyitch himself.

V. Ilyitch understood people very well, as was natural. Once when I went into his study, I found a man who was backing to the door and bowing at the same time to V. Ilyitch, and V. I. continued his writing without raising his eyes.

"Do you know him?" he asked, pointing toward the door.

I said I had come into contact with him twice—over the "Universal Literature" business.

"Well?"

"An ignorant, uncultured person, I should say."

"H'm, h'm, a certain toady and probably a scoundrel. But this is the first time I have seen him, and I may be mistaken."

V. Ilyitch was not mistaken. Several months later this man justified Lenin's description to the full.

He thought a lot about people because, as he said, "Our apparatus is very unsteady. Since October many elements have crept in. Your pious and beloved intelligentsia are to blame for that—it is the result of their mean sabotage."

He said this to me while we were walking in Gorky. I began speaking about Alexinsky, I don't remember why, probably he was up to one of his dirty tricks at the time.

"You can picture it to yourself. At our first meeting I had a feeling of physical repulsion toward him. I couldn't conquer it. No one has ever given me such a feeling before. We had to do some work together. I had to use every method to keep myself in check—it was very awkward. I felt—I simply cannot stand this degenerate."

Then, shrugging his shoulders in amazement, he said: "But I never saw through that scoundrel Malinovsky. That was a very mysterious affair, Malinovsky."

To me he was a strict teacher, and devoted friend.

"You are an enigmatic person," he said to me jokingly. "In literature you seem to be a good realist—and in your attitude to people, a romanticist. Are all people victims of history for you? We know history, and we say to the victims, 'Overturn the altars! Break down the temples! Down with the gods!' And you want to convince me that the militant party of the working class is bound first of all to make the intelligentsia comfortable."

I may be mistaken, but it seems to me that V. Ilyitch liked talking to me. He almost always suggested, "Come and see me—ring up, we will meet."

Once he said: "It's interesting to talk to you. You have a varied and wide circle of impressions." He would ask about the attitude of the intelligentsia, he was especially interested in the scientists. At that time I was working with N. B. Khalatov on the Committee for Improving the Conditions of the Scientists.

Proletarian Literature

He was interested in proletarian literature. "What do you think will come of it?"

I said that I expected a great deal, but considered it necessary to organize a *Litvuz* (institute for the study of literature), with chairs of philology, foreign languages—Western and Oriental—of folklore, of the history of universal literature, and of Russian literature separately.

"H'm, h'm," he said screwing up his eyes and chuckling. "Very wide and very dazzling! I am not against its being wide—but if it is to be dazzling—eh? We haven't professors of our own for these subjects, and the bourgeois professors will teach history of a sort. No, I don't think we must set about that yet. We must wait three or five years."

Then he would complain, "Have absolutely no time for reading!" He frequently and with strong emphasis referred to the value of Demyan Bedny's work for propaganda, but added: "It is somewhat crude. He follows the reader whereas he ought to be a little way ahead."

He mistrusted Mayakovsky, and was even rather irritated by him. "He shouts, invents some sort of distorted words, and doesn't get anywhere in my opinion—and besides is incomprehensible. It is all disconnected, difficult to read. He is talented? Very talented even? H'm, h'm. We shall see. But doesn't it seem to you that people are writing a lot of poetry now? There are whole pages of it in the newspapers and volumes of it appear every day."

I remarked that it was natural for youth to be attracted to poetry at such a time, and that in my opinion it is easier to write mediocre verse than good prose, and poetry takes less time. In addition we have many good teachers of the art of versifying.

"I don't believe it's easier to write verse than prose. I can't imagine it. I couldn't write two lines of poetry if you flayed me alive." Then he frowned. "We must spread among the masses all the old revolutionary literature—all that we have here and in Europe."

He was a Russian who lived for a long time away from his native land, and had examined it attentively —from afar it appears brighter and more beautiful. He estimated accurately its potential forces, and the exceptional talents of its people, which were as yet feebly expressed, unawakened by a monotonous and oppressive history, but which gleamed everywhere like golden stars against the somber background of the fantastic life of Russia.

Vladimir Lenin, profoundly and greatly a man of this world, is dead. His death is a grievous blow to the hearts of those who knew him, grievous indeed.

But the darkness of death only emphasizes the more strongly to the world his great importance as the leader of the working class of the world.

And if the dark cloud of hatred, of lies and calumny, were even denser than it is, it would matter not at all. There is no force which can put out the torch which Lenin raised aloft in the stifling darkness of a mad world.

And no other man has so well deserved the eternal remembrance of the world.

Vladimir Lenin is dead. But the inheritors of his thought and will are alive. They live and carry on a work which is more victorious than any other in the history of mankind.

BIOGRAPHICAL NOTES

ALEXINSKY, G. A. (born 1879).—Active since 1905 in the Russian Social-Democratic Party; member of the II Duma; during the war an ultra social-patriot; after the Bolshevik Revolution chief publicity agent for the White Guard General Wrangel.

ANDREYEVA, M. F.—Gorky's wife.

AXELROD, Paul B. (1850-1928).—Together with Plekhanov founded the first organized Marxist group, the Emancipation of Labor Group in 1883; later one of the foremost Menshevik leaders; bitter opponent of the Soviet Government; conducted an active campaign against Communism; member of the International Socialist Bureau of the Second International.

BAZAROV, V. A. (born 1874).—Russian economist and philosophical essayist; member of the Bolshevik Party until 1907 when he became a Machist; at present works in the State Planning Commission of the U.S.S.R.

BEBEL, August (1840-1913).—One of the founders and leaders of the German Social-Democratic Party.

BEDNY, Demyan (born 1883).—Satirical poet, Communist, and one of the most popular Russian writers.

BOGDANOV, A. A. (born 1873).—A well-known Bolshevik writer who joined the Machist group in 1908. At present head of Institute for Blood Transfusion in Moscow.

BUKHARIN, Nikolai I. (born 1889).—Prominent Bolshevik; leader of the recent Right Opposition in the Soviet Union, which he later renounced.

CHALIAPIN, Feodor (born 1873).—Famous Russian singer.

DAN, Theodore (born 1871).—Menshevik leader; during the war a pacifist; active in anti-Soviet propaganda abroad.

DEBS, Eugene V. (1855-1926).—Revolutionary trade unionist and Socialist propagandist, and one of the founders of the Socialist Party in the United States; four times candidate for president, warm supporter of the Bolshevik Revolution, bitter opponent of imperialist war for which he was convicted during the war to ten years of imprisonment. Failed to break with the Socialist Party after it had completely deserted Marxism.

DEUTSCH, Leo G. (born 1855).—One of the founders of the Emancipation of Labor Group in Russia in 1883; during the war an extreme chauvinist and co-worker of Plekhanov in 1917.

DÜRER, Albert (1471-1528).—A German painter, engraver and writer.

DZERZHINSKY, Felix (1877-1926).—One of the oldest members of Polish Social-Democracy; member of Bolshevik Central Committee from 1917 to his death; was chairman of the Tcheka, Commissar of Internal Affairs, Commissar of Communications, and President of the Supreme Economic Council.

FERRI, Enrico (1866-1929).—Italian Socialist, University lecturer, criminologist and lawyer.

HILLQUIT, Morris (born 1870).—One of the founders and leaders of the Socialist Party; wealthy lawyer; centrist and pacifist during the war; bitter opponent of the Soviet régime and Communism, and supporter of counter-revolutionary movements against the Soviet Union. Outstanding Right-Wing Socialist in America.

DAYS WITH LENIN 63

JAURÈS, Jean (1859-1914).—Outstanding French Socialist leader; assassinated at the outbreak of World War by a fanatic jingoist.

KAMENEV, L. B. (born 1883).—Old Bolshevik leader who, after the Revolution, occupied various Government posts; removed from posts and expelled from the Communist Party for organizing opposition, which he later renounced and was readmitted into Party.

KAUTSKY, Karl (born 1854).—Leading Marxian theoretician before the war; developing as a centrist yet before the imperialist war, he forsook Marxism altogether and became a social-pacifist during the war; bitter opponent of Soviet Government and Communist movement.

KHALATOV, N. B.—Formerly head of the State Publishing House (Gosisdat) of the Soviet Union.

KOLLANTAY, Alexandra M. (born 1872).—First worked with the Mensheviks and active in women's movement; during the war took an internationalist position and joined the Bolsheviks; has been engaged in Soviet diplomatic service abroad.

KRASSIN, L. B. (1870-1926).—Old Bolshevik leader, intrusted with many important Government posts after the October Revolution; was Soviet ambassador to England and to France.

LADYZHNIKOV, S. P.—Head of a publishing firm before the Revolution of 1917.

LUNACHARSKY, Anatol (born 1875).—Old Bolshevik; accomplished linguist, dramatist and literary critic; together with Bogdanov and others formed center of group disagreeing with Bolshevik leaders on fundamental philosophical problems; rejoined Bolshevik Party after the March Revolution; was People's Commissar of Education for many years.

LUXEMBURG, Rosa (1871-1919).—One of the outstanding revolutionary Socialist leaders and theoreticians; participated in German, Polish and Russian labor movements; imprisoned during the war; one of the founders of the Spartacus League which later became the Communist Party of Germany; assassinated together with Karl Liebknecht by German officers.

MALINOVSKY, Andrew.—Active in the Bolshevik Party since 1911; elected member of the IV Duma and to the Central Committee of the Party; although suspected for some time, was exposed as member of tsarist secret police from records obtained after the February Revolution; voluntarily returned to Russia after establishment of Soviet Government; was tried and executed as a traitor and spy.

MARTOV, L. (1873-1923).—Leader of Mensheviks; during the war a pacifist; during the first part of the Russian Revolution disagreed with the majority of his Party but later passed into the camp of the enemies of the Soviet Government.

MAYAKOVSKY, V. (1894-1930).—A leading Russian Futurist, "left front" poet after the October Revolution; committed suicide.

MEHRING, Franz (1846-1919).—Outstanding revolutionary Marxist historian and journalist; member of the Left Wing of the German Social-Democratic Party and one of the leaders of the Spartacus League.

MÜNZER, Thomas (1498-1526).—Leader of the peasant insurrection in Germany in 1525.

PARVUS (A. L. Helfand, 1869-1924).—Well-known Marxian theoretician; Russian political emigrant, active in the German Social-Democracy since the late nineties; during the war an extreme social chauvinist and agent of German imperialism engaged in various commercial enterprises connected with war contracts.

PLEKHANOV, George V. (1850-1918).—Founder of Marxian Socialism in Russia and Marxist theoretician; first a co-worker with Lenin, later

Menshevik leader; during war supported Russia's imperialist aims and after the October Revolution bitter opponent of Soviet Government.

SINGER, Paul (1844-1911).—With Bebel, one of the leaders of the German Social-Democracy.

TCHAIKOVSKY, N. (1860-1926).—Founder of one of the early Populist revolutionary groups in Russia; leader of the Social-Revolutionaries; social-patriot during World War; head of counter-revolutionary government in the North of Russia during the Civil War.

TOMSKY, M. P. (born 1880).—Bolshevik from youth; took active part in revolutions of 1905 and 1917. Was chairman of Central Council of Labor Unions of U.S.S.R. and of Central Committee of the Party since 1919; removed from leading posts for organizing Right Opposition; at present head of the State Publishing House.

TROTSKY, L. D. (born 1879).—After the split in the Russian Social-Democratic Party in 1903 remained with the Mensheviks; during the War an internationalist with leanings towards the Kautsky group; after the February Revolution joined the Bolshevik Party; member of Central Committee; held responsible Government posts; expelled from the Party in 1927 for leading opposition to Party program and policies, and removed from all posts. Later expelled from Soviet Union for organising underground anti-Soviet activities.

VOROVSKY, V. V. (1871-1923).—Old Bolshevik and one of the most prominent members of the Communist Party of the Soviet Union. Assassinated in 1923 while acting as Soviet representative at the Lausanne Conference.

ZHITLOVSKY, C.—Russian lecturer and writer; Social-Revolutionary; at present resides in New York.